# Nature's Children

# GAZELLES

**Sheila Dalton**

GROLIER
EDUCATIONAL

# FACTS IN BRIEF

### Classification of Gazelles

Class:     *Mammalia* (mammals)
Order:     *Artiodactyla*
Family:    *Bovidae*
Genus:    *Gazella;* several antelopes of other genera are also commonly considered gazelles.
Species: There are about 12 species of gazelles.

**World distribution.**    Mongolia and India to Egypt and Morocco and into eastern and central tropical Africa.

**Habitat.**    Open plains, mountains and bush.

**Distinctive physical characteristics.**    Slender body and long thin legs with two-toed hoofs. In most species male and female have black-ringed horns. Coat is brown with white undersides and rump, and black and white markings on face. Ears are long and narrow, and tail is short.

**Habits.**    Gazelles often graze in herds of up to several hundred. They are very fast runners.

**Diet.**    Grass, herbs, leaves and roots.

**Published originally as**
**"Getting to Know . . . Nature's Children."**

This series is approved and recommended by the Federation of Ontario Naturalists.

This library reinforced edition is available exclusively from:

GROLIER
EDUCATIONAL

**Sherman Turnpike, Danbury, Connecticut 06816**

# Contents

Everyone agrees that gazelles are among the world's most graceful animals, but did you know that they are also very, very fast? Some can reach speeds of over 80 kilometres (50 miles) an hour for 15 seconds or more. That's as fast as a car on a highway.

And did you know that gazelles belong to a group of animals known as antelopes? That won't surprise you if you know that the word antelope means bright-eyed, since a gazelle's large shining eyes are one of its most striking features.

To find out more about this beautiful and surprisingly hardy animal, just turn the page.

*Addra gazelle.*

# Where They Live

Opposite page:
*The unusual coloring on the face and long straight horns identify this animal as a Thomson's gazelle.*

Gazelles are found in Asia and Africa. Some make their home in mountainous regions, others in the desert or in shrubby areas known as the bush. Most live on grassy plains.

Whatever the area gazelles call home, it is always an open one, with very few places to hide. Often rain is seasonal, so at certain times of the year water is scarce. Fortunately, some gazelles — the Moroccan Dorcas, for instance — do not need to drink water at all.

They get the moisture they need from the roots and plants they eat.

Other gazelles are not so lucky. They do need to drink, and they depend on their speed and endurance to travel great distances to whatever watering holes they can find.

*The shaded area on this map shows where gazelles are found.*

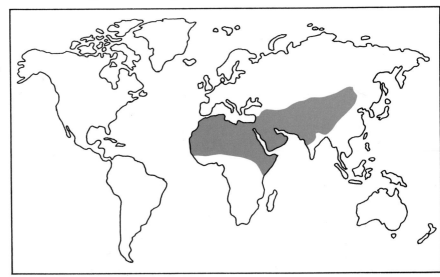

## Big and Little

There are at least ten different kinds of gazelles and some zoologists list as many as eighteen. Most have sandy brown coats with white undersides and rumps. Many have black and white markings on their faces and a horizontal dark band along each side. Their long pointed ears and large eyes give them a gentle appearance. Most have long V- or S-shaped horns.

The smallest gazelle is the Dorcas gazelle. It is not much bigger than a medium-sized dog, averaging 53 centimetres (21 inches) at the shoulder. The largest is the Dama gazelle, which is about the size of a Great Dane. But the gazelle's long neck, long horns and long, slender legs make it look much taller.

*The small yet elegant Dorcas gazelle.*

## Groups of Gazelles

Generally speaking, gazelles live in herds. Although a male, or buck, will wander alone at times, he is usually trying to establish a territory. Then he will mark out a large area of land as his own, and be joined by a group of females, or does. Usually, these females do not stay very long, but they are soon replaced by a new group. When a herd of does stay with a male longer than a few days, it is known as a harem. But harems move on too after a few weeks or months. Does and their young make up another kind of herd. Bachelors, too, hang around together. There are also mixed groups of both sexes and all ages. These usually form outside the breeding season and can range in size from three to ten thousand or more.

*The horns of these Grant's gazelles may grow to be as long as these animals are tall.*

# Gazelle Grub

Gazelles are browsers and grazers. This means that sometimes they eat grass, herbs and woody plants on the ground (graze), and sometimes they munch on the leaves, buds and shoots of trees and shrubs (browse). Some may also use their hoofs to dig up roots.

Just like other antelopes, and even cows, gazelles are ruminants, or cud-chewers. They swallow their food mainly unchewed and then bring it back to their mouth later to chew it more thoroughly. This allows them to eat quickly wherever they can find food — maybe under the watchful eye of a predator. Then they can chew it at their leisure afterwards, somewhere safer.

*To reach an out-of-the-way treat this gerenuk simply stands on its back legs and stretches its long neck.*

## Horns-a-Plenty

*Gazelle horns*

*Tibetan gazelle*

*Dama gazelle*

*Goitered gazelle*

One of the first things you notice about a gazelle is its magnificent set of horns.

A gazelle's horns are usually long, pointed and slender, with thickenings that form black rings at regular intervals. They can be straight, or curved forward or back, but they never have branches. Unlike a deer whose antlers are shed every year and replaced with a new set, a gazelle keeps its horns throughout its life. The core of the horn is an outgrowth of bone that begins at the gazelle's skull. The core is covered in keratin — the same stuff that your fingernails are made of. One of the most amazing things about a gazelle's horns is that they never stop growing.

In African gazelles, both males and females usually have horns. The female's horns are often shorter and thinner than those of the male, however. In most Asian gazelles, only the male has horns.

*The springbuck is a beautiful gazelle with curving horns, long ears and large eyes surrounded by long lashes.*

14

## When Push Comes to Shove

Although a gazelle's horns can look fairly threatening, they are seldom actually used as weapons. Male gazelles mostly use them to show off, as if to say, "Hey, look at my horns! Aren't they something?" Often that's all it takes to scare off a rival. Even when two males do fight, they seldom hurt each other, and unless the fight is over a female, there is often no obvious winner or loser. The two bucks just lock horns, and push and twist and shove until one breaks away. Then one or both of them will just switch to another activity. A fight usually lasts no longer than five minutes, and is sometimes as short as a few seconds.

Gazelle fighting, in fact, is sometimes so tame that the opponents may not even touch each other at all! In "air-cushion-fighting," they face each other at a distance of a metre (yard) or two, go through all the motions of fighting, but never come into contact.

*Just letting off a bit of steam.*

*Gazelle Horns*

*Slender-horned gazelle*

*Dibatag*

*Blackbuck*

## Putting on a Show

Gazelle males rarely need to fight because they have other ways of letting one another know who's boss. A territorial male with a harem will often separate himself from the females, moving and grazing apart from them. This allows other males to see him from a distance. That's usually enough to keep them off his property.

When bucks do meet, the older or territorial one may do a number of things to tell the other "I'm in charge around here." For instance, he'll lift his nose so high his horns touch his back, or he'll turn his head quickly to one side. If this doesn't work, lowering his horns as if he's ready to fight does the trick. The younger or non-territorial male almost always backs down, dropping to his knees with head and neck stretched forward. Then he gets up and calmly goes about his business. He may not leave the territory, but for the time being at least, he will not try to take it away from its owner.

*A male gazelle on the watch as his harem feeds.*

## Staking Out a Territory

There comes a time in all male gazelles' lives when they feel the urge to establish their own territory. Many young bucks find and take over a territory that has been left vacant. In some species, a male seeks out a group of does and simply moves in. But sometimes a young buck must fight an older male in order to win his territory. Whoever loses has to move on.

You would think that after finding a place to call his own, a buck would hang on to it. But often he doesn't. He may just stop being territorial one day, sometimes after as little as two months. In some cases, the females move out and the buck is left alone. He may then join a mixed herd or a group of wandering bachelors before establishing a territory again later. Many bucks repeat this cycle several times.

However short-lived, territoriality serves a purpose. The male provides protection for does and young. He also has many females to mate with. This means that more strong young are born, which helps the species to survive.

*A trio of Grant's gazelles on the alert.*

## Home on the Range

Once he's on his own turf, a buck has a rather odd way of making himself at home. He goes to the middle of his territory and drops some dung. He does this every day until quite a heap has formed. This seems to be his version of putting up a sign with his name on it.

Bucks also mark their territories with urine, and in many species they use glands just beneath their eyes as well. These glands are called the preorbital glands. A buck will carefully lower his head until the gland comes into contact with a blade of grass, depositing a secretion that hardens in the open air. Does have these glands, too, but only the males mark objects with them.

Sometimes a passing male will sniff the mark, then leave one of his own nearby — a kind of calling card to say he's stopped by. All these marking behaviors help the buck become familiar with his territory, while at the same time keeping him in communication with other males.

*You can tell this Dorcas gazelle is a young one because its horns are quite small and it has not yet acquired the striking colors of the adults.*

# Cool, Calm and Collected

Overleaf:
*Roosevelt's
gazelles.*

For an animal that seems to go out of its way to avoid a fight, gazelles have a lot of enemies. Lions, leopards, hyenas, cheetahs and wild dogs hunt and kill adult gazelles. In Asia, wolves are a major danger. Pythons can swallow small gazelles whole, after wrapping themselves around them and cutting off their breathing. Jackals, baboons and tawny eagles also prey upon fawns.

With all these dangers to face, you'd expect gazelles to be a nervous bunch. But they actually live and eat very peacefully. A herd will get upset if one of them is captured and killed, but it quickly settles down again. And gazelles do not even react to a predator unless it is really a threat. If a lion passes by, for instance, the herd will pay no attention to it at all unless it is obvious that the lion is hunting and going to attack. This way, the gazelles save energy for those times when they do have to run for their lives.

# A Friend in Need

An animal with so many enemies needs good friends as well — and luckily, gazelles have some.

East African oxpeckers, a kind of starling, prowl the bodies of gazelles in search of ticks, maggots and bloodsucking flies. They even clean up any open wounds a gazelle may have. Gazelles can often be seen turning their heads and holding their ears steady so that an oxpecker can reach in and peck out a bug or two. And when danger threatens, the oxpecker always runs to the side facing away from the enemy before flying away. This alerts the gazelle to the direction in which danger is approaching.

Zebras and giraffes often share feeding areas and watering holes with gazelles. They help each other because they have different strengths. Although gazelles have good eyesight, zebras and giraffes can spot an enemy before they can. On the other hand, gazelles have keener noses and sharper ears, and they smell or hear danger before either of the other two.

Opposite page: *The giraffe is a friendly watchtower for any nearby gazelles, alerting them to dangers only it can see far in the distance.*

## Keeping Out of Trouble

A gazelle is actually well protected against danger. In addition to super senses, it has a coat that blends in with its surroundings, making it hard for an enemy to see.

Some gazelles with striped flanks shake them before running away from an enemy. This warns the rest of the herd of danger. Others lift up their tails in a flash of white, and some sound the alarm with a loud snort. This tells nearby gazelles to stop everything and run.

Generally, gazelles are not strong enough to fight their enemies. Their best defense is to run. But instead of running in a straight line, they zigzag. That way, the predator never knows where they're headed next. Gazelles have even been seen jumping straight over lions that were rushing right at them.

*The Thomson's gazelle is one of the most common animals of eastern Africa's plains.*

## Spotted and Stotted

Gazelles have another very clever way of dealing with enemies. It's called stotting, and it works so well that it's one big reason they don't need to run away whenever a predator appears.

Stotting refers to a gazelle's way of leaping high in the air with its legs stiff and its back arched. Zoologists now think that this strange bouncing behavior is gazelle-talk for "You've been spotted. Don't bother trying to sneak up on me." Most predators know that healthy gazelles can outrun them. If they can't surprise one, they won't bother chasing it.

They might, however, give chase to an old or weak gazelle, and stotting may transmit another message as well: "See how fit and strong I am!" If the predator had any thought of being able to win a race with this gazelle, it now knows it is hopelessly outmatched.

*Stotting springbuck*

*"Run!"*

## Helpful Herds

When it comes to safety and protection, the herd itself serves a useful function. In a herd, there is always someone acting as a look-out. A herd has hundreds, sometimes thousands, of eyes, ears and noses to help spot an enemy. Also, it is hard for a predator to isolate a single animal in a herd. In a mass of animals, a hungry lion or wild dog has less room to move about and is hampered in its attack. A victim can escape by mingling in the crowd.

Moreover, predators always direct their attack against a single animal. But the herd makes this difficult to do. When a predator charges, the herd bursts out in all directions and the chosen victim disappears in the crowd. The enemy, its movements hampered by the milling mass of animals, gets confused and wastes time trying to home in on it again. Lions, in particular, are easily distracted this way. Unfortunately, cheetahs seem to be able to concentrate on one animal in a herd no matter what the others are doing.

*Safety in numbers.*

## Starting a Family

Gazelles mate all year round. Different species have different peak periods. For example, some gazelles breed so that most of the young are born during the rainy season, when food and water are plentiful.

To attract a doe's attention, a buck will put on a courtship display — he lifts his nose in the air and kicks his front legs straight out in front of him, like a soldier on parade. Sometimes, he puts his legs right under the female's belly. He'll also sniff her urine. If she is ready to mate, her urine has a certain smell only a male gazelle can appreciate.

If all goes well, she and the buck will then perform a mating march, with the doe in the lead. Mating itself is brief and, soon afterwards, the two go their separate ways.

*"Let's get acquainted."*

# Birth of a Fawn

About five to seven months after mating, depending on the species, the doe gives birth to a single baby, or fawn. In some species, the male stays close by her after the birth — but not because of the baby. He's really hoping to persuade the female to mate with him again.

Right after birth, the mother gazelle cleans her baby by licking it all over, from its head to its hoofs. She may be labeling the fawn with her own scent this way, so that she can find it again. For she will soon leave it on its own and rejoin the herd for a short while.

The licking also has a kind of "waking up" effect on the fawn. Within minutes, it struggles to its feet — sometimes with a helpful prod, or even a kick, from Mom. After it has nursed for a little while, it will move away to find a hiding place where its tawny coat blends in with its surroundings. There it will bed down until its mother calls it again for more nursing.

*A newborn gazelle gets a loving lick from its mother.*

## Practice Makes Perfect

The new baby will stay hidden for at least the first two weeks of its life. When Mom comes to nurse it, it will answer her cries and come out from its hiding place to meet her. Then, sometimes after a bit of nose-nuzzling, it settles down for a good meal.

After feeding comes playtime. The fawn bounces around its mother in circles, stopping only when it has to catch its breath. Then it starts all over again. At last it's had enough, and totters off to its hiding place.

As the fawn gets a little older, it sometimes plays at fighting. When its mother approaches, it lowers its head. If Mom then lowers hers in response to this "threat," the fawn scampers around in delight, carried away with the fun of it all. Without realizing it, the youngster is learning and practicing for when it grows up.

*Staying well hidden until its mother calls.*

## Don't Mess with Mom

When it's about two to three weeks old, the young gazelle starts following its mother for longer and longer periods, slowly becoming a full-fledged member of the herd. That's when the doe's protective instincts really come into their own. Any predator that threatens her baby had better watch out! Normally gentle, mother gazelles have been known to attack jackals and baboons. One was even seen chasing a baboon for three hours after it had killed her fawn. A gazelle mom will sometimes charge people, too, if they get too close to her offspring.

Usually, though, gazelle moms will try to distract an enemy rather than attack it. When a fawn is too young to run fast, it will hide from a predator while its mother and other adults in the herd flee. This distracts the animal from the baby. Because adult gazelles run so fast, often nobody gets hurt.

*This young Saharan Dorcas gazelle will not be nursing for much longer. It's getting to be too big.*

# Adolescence

A young gazelle usually nurses for about four to six months. What seems to bring nursing to an end is the size of the fawn. Before, when it butted its head into its mother's belly to get the milk flowing, no harm was done. But now it's big enough to hurt and Mom starts avoiding it at feeding time.

Still, the two will stay together in the same herd for the time being. Soon, though, a young male may find himself being harassed by the adult buck that owns the territory. Clearly, the time has come for him to leave and join a bachelor herd. A young female often stays with her mother's herd at least until she is old enough to seek a mate of her own, usually when she is about 18 months old.

# Looking into the Future

In order for gazelles to continue to survive in Asia and Africa, people must make an effort to provide safe places for them to live. Right now, many of them are being killed by hunters and more and more of their grazing land is being turned into farms. Fortunately, efforts are being made by governments and individuals to protect the gazelle. Game reserves and national parks have been set up in many of the countries where they live, and the future is beginning to look brighter for these beautiful and graceful animals.

# Words to Know

**Antelopes**    A group of hoofed, cud-chewing mammals that includes gazelles.

**Antler**    Branched bony growth on the heads of deer and their relatives. Antlers are shed each year.

**Browse**    Feed on leaves and shoots of trees and shrubs.

**Buck**    A male gazelle.

**Cud**    Hastily swallowed food brought back for chewing by animals such as gazelles, deer and cows.

**Doe**    A female gazelle.

**Fawn**    A young gazelle.

**Graze**    Feed on grass and plants on the ground.

**Harem**    Herd of female gazelles that gathers and stays some time in a male's territory.

**Horn**    A bony outgrowth on the head of gazelles, other antelopes, sheep, cattle and goats. Horns are not shed and continue to grow throughout the animal's life.

**Keratin**    Protein that forms the basis of horns, nails, feathers, hair and scales.

**Predator**    An animal that hunts other animals for food.

**Ruminant**    An animal that chews the cud, including antelopes, cows, sheep and camels.

**Stotting**    A high stiff-legged jump characteristic of gazelles. Also called *pronking*.

**Territory**    Area that an animal or group of animals lives in and often defends from other animals of the same kind.

# INDEX

**Cover Photo:**   Stephen J. Krasemann (Peter Arnold, Inc.)
**Photo Credits:**   Zoological Society of San Diego, pages 4, 24, 25, 43; Steven C. Kaufman (Peter Arnold, Inc.), page 7; John Newby (WWF-Photolibrary, page 8; Breck P. Kent, pages 11, 16; Stan Bain, page 12; Phyllis Greenberg, pages 15, 35; Gerald & Buff Corsi, pages 19, 31, 36; Sandved & Coleman Photography, pages 20, 32; Nancy Adams, page 23; Bill Ivy, page 27; Barry Dursley, page 28; Klaus Paysan (Peter Arnold, Inc.), page 39; George W. Frame (WWF-Photolibrary), page 40.